CHILD CARE INSTITUTE
POST OFFICE BOX 3624
SILVER SPRINGS, MD 20901

SURVIVAL KIT FOR EARLY CHILDHOOD DIRECTORS

Solutions to daily problems
with staff, parents, children,
organization, environment

Early Childhood
Directors Association

Illustrations by
Ellen Krans

Published by: Toys'n Things Press
a division of Resources for Child Caring, Inc.
906 North Dale Street
St. Paul, Minnesota 55103

Distributed by: Gryphon House
P.O. Box 275
Mount Rainier, MD 20712

Acropolis Books Ltd.
2400 17th Street N.W.
Washington, D.C. 20009

ISBN: 0-934140-24-3

Library of Congress Catalog Card Number: 88-24944

Printed in the United States of America

Acknowledgements

SURVIVAL KIT FOR EARLY CHILDHOOD DIRECTORS is a compilation of resources from many people who submitted their ideas and/or services. We would like to express our appreciation to the following people:

- Members of the Early Childhood Directors Association who submitted the ideas used in this book:

Stella Bowland	Cathy Mears
Phyllis Ettinger	Marlys Nelson
Sister Francette	Daphyn Nordeen
Janet Harmon	Mary Jo Olson
Ginger Hause	Rhoda Redleaf
Michelle Kessler	Kathleen Reidell
Pat Landy	Jackie Spies
Alice Marks	Betsy Townsend

- Rhoda Redleaf and Mary Jo Olson for writing and editing;
- Ellen Krans for cover design and illustrations;
- Gerri Maruk and Denise Schoster for typing;
- Sue Baldwin for editing and production management;
- Jean Nicol for her help and continuous support;
- Susan Middleton and Beth Overstad for final proofreading and editing.

Contents

Introduction

The Early Childhood Directors Association is a professional organization serving ninety-five nursery school and day care directors in the greater St. Paul area of Minnesota. The sharing of creative ideas and experiences has been a function of the group since its inception. Through mutual support and the constantly improving skills of our members, the Early Childhood Directors Association makes a positive contribution to the quality of child care in our community. The ideas contained in this book are but the tip of an iceberg compared to the collective wisdom of ninety-five directors! As much as each one of us knows, there is always so much more to learn from each other, and thus we now are pleased to share this information with other directors throughout the country.

We certainly hope the **SURVIVAL KIT FOR DIRECTORS** proves useful to you and helps make your job a bit easier and better!

Staff Management

PROBLEM AREA: BECOMING PART OF AN EXISTING SYSTEM

SPECIFIC INCIDENT:
Long-time staff members expressed a concern that new staff members did not fully understand the workings of the school. Their roles, responsibilities and the program philosophy needed clarification.

HOW WAS IT SOLVED?:
An employee handbook was developed which covered the following areas: hiring and employment issues (i.e., benefits, payroll, training requirements, separation, promotion, absences and holidays); philosophy and goals of program; communication issues (i.e., parents, staff, children and community); guidelines for roles and responsibilities; health procedures and safety steps; and materials and environment (i.e., use of equipment and supplies, goals and guidelines for interest areas).

STEPS IN IMPLEMENTATION:
1. Long-term staff members were asked to help in the preparation of the handbook, so their concerns were included. Board members also helped.
2. A portion of staff meetings were devoted to work on the handbook. People volunteered to work on various sections. The director compiled material and asked for added input before completion.
3. The handbook was distributed at a staff workshop prior to beginning of the school year. Long-time staff members assisted in the discussion and presentation of the handbook. As the year progressed, a list of items to be added to the handbook was developed.

COMMENTS:
This handbook is also given to all student teachers and new staff members prior to their starting to work in the program. This helps them better understand the program philosophy and their role. During their orientation, the director discusses the handbook and answers any of their questions.

PROBLEM AREA: STAFFING PATTERNS

SPECIFIC INCIDENT:

Early morning and late afternoon shifts were rotated. Some staff were continually late in the morning while others were very tired late in the day.

HOW WAS IT SOLVED?:

The staff were allowed to choose the shifts they wished to work. Most people know their own energy level and select the times they prefer to work.

STEPS IN IMPLEMENTATION:

1. The director discussed the problem with the staff and asked people to indicate the hours they preferred to regularly work. The director took responsibility for working out staffing patterns based on their preferences. Rotations were to be scheduled only if there were times no one wanted to work.
2. As it turned out, the early morning and late afternoon people balanced out so the whole day could be covered very nicely without a rotation system.
3. The same principle was applied to some of the specific activities during the day. Some high energy people enjoyed doing active tasks such as exercise, creative movement, and outdoor play and disliked naptime, and story time. The director encouraged staff to cooperate in working out balances they liked.

COMMENTS:

Now, a few people are regularly the first ones to go outdoors, while others prefer the dressing and cleaning up tasks. Some staff choose extra naptime and backrub sessions to balance out taking their break during gym period. The staff is happier and the children are getting better programming since the staff was permitted to choose their own special activities and times.

PROBLEM AREA: LACK OF PROFESSIONAL RESOURCES

SPECIFIC INCIDENT:

A teacher wanted some books on discipline to help with a problem, but the center didn't have the ones she mentioned and couldn't afford to buy them.

HOW WAS IT SOLVED?:

A library was set up using books that staff members were willing to bring in and share.

STEPS IN IMPLEMENTATION:

1. Many teachers had purchased various books of their own and were frequently bringing them in for each other anyway.
2. The staff decided to formalize the system and encourage people to bring in books to establish a professional library for the teachers.
3. The staff wrote their names in their books and turned in a master list of the books they loaned to the library. A sign-out sheet for the books was used and a two-week limit for check-out was established. A shelf of reserve books to be used only in the center was also established.

COMMENTS:

The library was put in the staff lounge so people could browse through books on breaks or at naptime. A kitty of contributions and fines for late books was initiated. The money is used to purchase books for the center and to replace any books that get lost. People have been very responsible about taking care of the books and really appreciate having them available. This system does a lot for professional development and morale in the center.

PROBLEM AREA: PROFESSIONAL DEVELOPMENT TIME

SPECIFIC INCIDENT:

Time was needed for staff orientation sessions and the director wanted to encourage and facilitate staff attendance at annual professional conferences.

HOW WAS IT SOLVED?:

A policy of closing the center at set times each year was implemented to allow for professional development.

STEPS IN IMPLEMENTATION:

1. An annual calendar is planned which includes professional development days. Specifically, this breaks down into one week in August for orientation and teacher work days prior to the opening of school and one day in October for a professional conference.
2. The calendar is given to all parents prior to registration so they know teacher time off is part of the school policy. It is best to distribute the calendar at the beginning of the school year and announce days off to currently-enrolled parents well in advance of the first time the center will be closed.
3. Initially the staff offered to assist people in finding alternative care, but when it is announced well in advance people can usually make their own arrangements.

COMMENTS:

Most parents appreciate sending their child or children to a center that is staffed by professionals. They have come to accept teachers' professional growth and work days as part of the public school calendar as well.

PROBLEM AREA: INAPPROPRIATE USE OF SICK LEAVE

SPECIFIC INCIDENT:

Some staff appeared to be abusing sick leave by calling in sick when they were not sick, but had to be away from work for other reasons. This meant a last minute substitute had to be found.

HOW WAS IT SOLVED?:

The "sick leave" policy was changed to a more general type of leave. Staff are allowed five days annual leave after the three month probation period, and ten days annual leave after the first fifteen months. Leave can be used as they see fit. Appropriate uses of leave are doctor or dental appointments, care of a sick child, or a mental health day. Leave can be requested in advance, making it much easier to plan for substitutes. Staff are allowed no more than two days at a time for scheduled non-sick leaves.

STEPS IN IMPLEMENTATION:

1. Employees are informed of the leave policy when they are hired.
2. Initially the staff was involved in the decision to develop this annual leave policy. They were in favor of it and provided valuable suggestions in planning the details of what should be allowed.

COMMENTS:

Since implementing this policy, there is no problem with staff members needing a day off and calling in sick when they are not actually sick. Staff ask far in advance so a substitute can be found. Recognition of the need for a mental health day makes employees feel the director does understand the stress involved with their position. Child caring programs in particular should certainly allow their staff to use sick days for their own children's sickness. Teachers have even located on-call substitutes if their child is running a high fever in the evening and they anticipate the possibility of being absent the next day.

PROBLEM AREA: IN-SERVICE TRAINING

SPECIFIC INCIDENT:

The busy schedules of staff members sometimes made it difficult to plan in-service training sessions for everyone during the normal work time.

HOW WAS IT SOLVED?:

Observation of other centers were scheduled during work hours. Staff members went individually or in pairs.

STEPS IN IMPLEMENTATION:

1. Staff members choose 1-3 centers to observe and make the arrangements two weeks in advance. This allows the director time to schedule substitutes as needed and to adjust the schedule. Staff are strongly encouraged to go at times when extra help is available or there is lighter enrollment.
2. Up to three hours paid time is allowed for this and it is counted as in-service. Staff are usually encouraged to visit at least two centers and divide the time rather than spending all three hours in one center.
3. The staff shares observations with others at staff meetings.

COMMENTS:

Staff members return with many new ideas, and usually with a good feeling about the present program. Paid time is an incentive, and a fun way to fulfill in-service needs. Sometimes particular types of visits are encouraged and staff are asked to observe specific procedures such as meals, naps, or other areas which might be of particular benefit to those staff members. This is very useful when re-evaluating center routines.

PROBLEM AREA: ANNUAL WORK SCHEDULES

SPECIFIC INCIDENT:

The staff was constantly asking for special days off for things such as personal needs, family needs, or trips.

HOW WAS IT SOLVED?:

The staff was given the option of working a flexible calendar of 170 to 190 days. In August, the staff marks on their attendance forms the days they plan to be off, if any, during the year.

STEPS IN IMPLEMENTATION:

1. The staff sign up in August and schedule their leaves based on the number of days they plan to work.
2. They cooperate on scheduling since everyone knows ahead of time when others want time off.
3. They also have the option of making arrangements with staff on other shifts who might want to cover and work extra days.

COMMENTS:

This system works well and results in less burn-out among staff members. They have the option of altering their schedules from year to year, working less time or half-time during summer months or holiday seasons. There is no friction among staff members over time off as the schedule incorporates most people's needs. Everyone gets the same holidays when school is closed as well as the specific number of vacation days they are entitled to, but there is less pressure on scheduling personal vacation days at set times because of the options this flexible system offers. Substitutes can be scheduled well in advance.

PROBLEM AREA: <u>EVALUATING THE DIRECTOR'S PERFORMANCE</u>

SPECIFIC INCIDENT:
There were many complaints by board members about the director's job performance.

HOW WAS IT SOLVED?:
The director began setting annual written goals and getting board approval for them.

STEPS IN IMPLEMENTATION:
1. The director used the center's mission statement and the job description to plan a series of goals and objectives.
2. The board was given the chance to respond, ask questions, and add ideas.
3. The personel committee then had something on which to base the year-end evaluation of the director.
4. Each goal was put somewhere on the calendar to establish a time by which the goal was to be completed.

COMMENTS:
The director also began preparing a monthly <u>written</u> "Director's Report to the Board" regarding monthly enrollment, finances, events, and progress toward goals and objectives.

PROBLEM AREA: LOW MORALE

SPECIFIC INCIDENT:

The staff as a whole seemed to be in a slump and morale was low.

HOW WAS IT SOLVED?:

A rotating "treat schedule" was established. A designated staff member brings a treat on Friday. The treat is set on the table in the lounge with a note from the "treater."

STEPS IN IMPLEMENTATION:

1. Interest the staff in the plan. It helps to make it optional.
2. Post a staff sign-up schedule on a bulletin board so everyone knows when they're responsible.
3. Begin! It may help to have the director start the process by being the first treater and doing something that is creative and fun for everyone.

COMMENTS:

The notes from the "treater" are fun to read. They can be simple or include more complicated ideas such as puzzles or riddles. Treats can be cheese and crackers, fruit, or baked goods. Even ice cream was served in the summer. Anything goes! People have decorated the lounge, written messages on balloons, and instituted a scavenger hunt for clues to find the treat.

PROBLEM AREA: UNEVENLY BALANCED WORKLOAD

SPECIFIC INCIDENT:

The staff expressed feelings that the workload was unevenly distributed.

HOW WAS IT SOLVED?:

The director organized staff meetings with productivity and distribution of work as the topics for the agenda.

STEPS IN IMPLEMENTATION:

1. The staff meeting was planned.
2. Prior to the meeting, the staff submitted ideas they felt might address the problem.
3. All ideas were discussed. It was decided the top two items would be implemented immediately.
4. An evaluation was done.
5. Additional ideas were implemented when possible.

COMMENTS:

The staff felt a part of this decision-making process, so the outcome was very positive.

PROBLEM AREA: STAFF MOTIVATION

SPECIFIC INCIDENT:

The dilemma concerned motivating exceptional employees when all staff in a specific job category were paid the same wage.

HOW WAS IT SOLVED?:

A combination cost of living/merit raise was instituted and a salary schedule for each job position was established.

STEPS IN IMPLEMENTATION:

1. The director conducted three formal observations of each staff member during the year.
2. Each observation report was discussed with the staff member and suggestions for improvement were talked over.
3. Annual performance evaluations were conducted using the information from observations as well as the staff member's self-evaluation and director's evaluation.

COMMENTS:

Aides, assistant teachers, teachers and head teachers all have a 5-step salary schedule for their positions. A person is always hired at the first or second level. After the annual evaluation in the spring, each staff member gets a written evaluation and is notified if they will be rehired for the fall, and whether they will receive a one-step increase (a no increase or a half-step increase is possible in certain cases). The salary schedule receives an annual cost of living raise.

PROBLEM AREA: <u>INADEQUATE CUSTODIAL SERVICE</u>

SPECIFIC INCIDENT:

The bathrooms could never pass inspections by the Department of Public Welfare.

HOW WAS IT SOLVED?:

It was decided that if the custodian understood <u>why</u> specific tasks needed to be done, he would be more cooperative.

STEPS IN IMPLEMENTATION:

1. The custodian was given a list of the Department of Public Welfare's regulations regarding standards of cleanliness.
2. He was asked to read the regulations and state how the center met the standards, and what needed to be done to keep in compliance with the law.
3. The director also asked what he needed, if anything, to help him meet these standards.

COMMENTS:

The custodian whom we had considered an adversary became "part of the team" when he understood that the staff wasn't being demanding, but had specific needs that he could help fill!

PROBLEM AREA: STAFF ILLNESSES

SPECIFIC INCIDENT:

1. The teacher who normally opened the center was sick and needed a substitute.
2. On another occasion, the second person scheduled to arrive was not able to come in, which left the opening person alone until the third scheduled person arrived.

HOW WAS IT SOLVED?:

1. The director arranged for a regular substitute who was available to fill in for the opening teacher and gave her an extra set of keys.
2. Any early morning staff person who is sick is required to call the next scheduled staff person and ask her or him to arrive half an hour early so the opening person will not be alone too long.

STEPS IN IMPLEMENTATION:

1. Find an opening substitute in the immediate neighborhood. This person need not be available all day, but must be extremely responsible and able to get to the center quickly to open in an emergency. Having an extra set of keys in the immediate neighborhood is very helpful, particularly if not all early morning staff have keys.
2. Inform the opening teacher of the name and phone number of the substitute and how early in the morning that person needs to be called.
3. Be sure all early morning staff have complete staff work schedules, plus the teachers' home phone numbers so they can alert them of a need to arrive earlier than usual.

COMMENTS:

Having a system in place to handle early morning emergencies saves lots of phone calls to the director at 4:00 or 5:00 in the morning.

PROBLEM AREA: SCHEDULING SUBSTITUTES

SPECIFIC INCIDENT:

The staff would call in sick, which meant the director had to find substitutes and make all the arrangements in the wee hours of the morning or rush to the center herself or himself, feeling resentful.

HOW WAS IT SOLVED?:

The director made the staff responsible for finding their own substitutes when they weren't going to be at work.

STEPS IN IMPLEMENTATION:

1. Develop a substitute list for all job levels.
2. Distribute the list at a staff meeting and explain the new procedure.
3. Be consistent and insist that staff find their own substitutes. Encourage them to make arrangements in advance instead of waiting until the very last minute.

COMMENTS:

Since the responsibility was now with the staff, the director stopped getting calls at home. There was resistance at first from staff, but more acceptance with time. They also began to make substitute arrangements in advance instead of waiting until the last minute. The director still gets an occasional call from a person who is extremely ill and has called a few people but has been unable to find someone.

PROBLEM AREA: LOW STAFF MORALE AND PRODUCTIVITY

SPECIFIC INCIDENT:

The staff were feeling low and lacked enthusiasm. They were going through activities in a very routine and uninspired manner and not making much effort. They felt their efforts were not really appreciated and were therefore slacking off in their jobs.

HOW WAS IT SOLVED?:

A new project was started, involving video-taping daily activities for parents to view.

STEPS IN IMPLEMENTATION:

1. The idea was shared with the staff to get their feedback and support. The staff was most enthusiastic about it, and eager to begin.
2. Staff members arranged for rental of the equipment for the times they wished to use it.
3. The staff took charge of scheduling filming. The director arranged times for staff and parental viewing. After the staff had reviewed and edited the tapes, different groups ran their tapes at arrival and pickup times (pickup worked better as parents were less rushed).

COMMENTS:

The staff really enjoyed learning about and using video equipment, taking turns filming and editing. The teachers were eager to plan special events to video-tape as well. It was a fun and valuable project that really boosted staff morale. Parents were very pleased with the opportunity to see what their child's typical day was like. They gave the teachers wonderful feedback about all they were doing which made the teachers feel much more appreciated. This project really promoted parental knowledge and support for the center.

PROBLEM AREA: STAFF MEETING ABSENCES

SPECIFIC INCIDENT:

The center has a number of part-time aides, who cover the naproom during staff meetings. Since these people were not able to attend staff meetings, the director was spending much time conveying information shared at the meetings to those who were not present.

HOW WAS IT SOLVED?:

The director decided to tape record staff meetings, particularly when necessary information was given or policies and procedures were decided upon.

STEPS IN IMPLEMENTATION:

1. The problem was shared with the staff, and they were told of plans to record staff meetings.
2. Everyone felt it was a good idea, but worried about people's reluctance to express concerns if they were being recorded. It was decided to turn the tape off for some discussions or at anyone's special request, remembering to turn the tape on again as needed.

COMMENTS:

This system has worked well. It gives a very complete record of staff meetings and has eliminated the need for someone to take extensive minutes, although someone still writes down action steps needed. Everyone who missed a meeting, or those who don't come to meetings (volunteers, students and part-timers) listen to the tapes to catch up on information. The director's weary brain is saved from needless information processing after meetings. By tape recording a set list of things to remember, there is no need for repetition when a new helper is being briefed.

PROBLEM AREA: STAFF MEETINGS

SPECIFIC INCIDENT:

With a large staff, some members felt free to dominate staff discussions while others rarely spoke.

HOW WAS IT SOLVED?:

In order to help each staff member express her or his own ideas, complaints, and suggestions, a "Staff Meeting Supplement" was implemented. It was to be filled out and handed in ahead of time, brought along to be shared at the meeting, or just used as a reminder of what that staff member wanted to bring up.

STEPS IN IMPLEMENTATION:

1. Create a simple form, with staff suggestions on the format.
2. Make sure each staff member has access to the form.
3. Remember to ask for the supplements at the beginning of each staff meeting and be sure to give positive reinforcement to the quiet people who suggest topics.

COMMENTS:

Many quiet staff members welcome the chance to write ideas down. Realize, however, that you are unlikely to change quiet people into active "talkers" with this method.

PROBLEM AREA: COMPLETING CHILD OBSERVATIONS

SPECIFIC INCIDENT:

As the staff prepared for conferences they did not have specific information on a few children. Regular observations had been discussed but they were not completed. Staff said that even though they wanted to do more observing, they didn't have enough time to watch and take notes on individual children.

HOW WAS IT SOLVED?:

A decision was made to develop some type of group observation form which would encourage staff to do some objective recording of what was happening with the children. The form introduced a systematic observation procedure that was not too time consuming.

STEPS IN IMPLEMENTATION:

1. A time-activity spot check form was developed. Many duplicate copies were made.
2. The form was explained at a staff meeting. Each teacher wrote the names of children in her group on one axis and the activities available in the room on the other.
3. To observe, they simply looked around the room and checked or made dots indicating what each child was doing. It took about one minute or less. There was room to write a quick comment about children as needed. Other codes were suggested to indicate the child's level of involvement, such as writing a "D" for Doing, "W" for Watching, or "NI" for not involved.

COMMENTS:

If used frequently, the form is quite effective. Teachers really enjoy using it and find it gives them lots of information to use during parent conferences. It is also useful in evaluating the environment. When some activities have very few or no marks by them, the staff knows that something needs to be changed in that area.

PROBLEM AREA: STAFF PROBLEM SOLVING

SPECIFIC INCIDENT:

Staff members were bringing the director problems they could and should have been solving themselves, such as problems with shared space, getting children ready for the bus, other scheduling issues.

HOW WAS IT SOLVED?:

A workshop on effective inter-staff communication and the use of "I" messages was conducted. The workshop was held in the evening and was required for all staff. The staff practiced stating their concerns in ways that did not make others defensive, but focused on solving the problem and expressing their feelings about the situation. A useful source for the staff workshop was "A Practical Approach to Resolving Inter-Staff Conflict" by Dr. Marjorie J. Kostelnick (*Child Care Information Exchange*, July/August, 1982, pp 7-12).

STEPS IN IMPLEMENTATION:

1. A workshop plan was developed and implemented.
2. Staff were told that inter-staff communication would be a part of their regular (on-going) evaluation.
3. Guidelines for effective communication were added to the "Employee Handbook."

COMMENTS:

The director rerouted back to the staff problems that were brought to her. Procedural problems did need to be resolved and situations needed to be defined as to which problems should be solved by those involved and which needed to be presented to the whole staff at a meeting. Staff were asked to define and clarify that issue as part of the workshop. Some staff needed coaching in using this method of communication after the workshop. Fewer problems are now coming to the director because the staff are working out problems on their own.

PROBLEM AREA: A.M.-P.M. STAFF COMMUNICATION

SPECIFIC INCIDENT:

Pertinent information about particular children was not shared between staff members. Occasionally parents would tell a teacher something that had upset, excited or affected their child (items not written in the sign-in log), or some event had happened during the morning that affected behavior, yet the information was not shared with other staff.

HOW WAS IT SOLVED?:

A staff log book was developed solely for the staff to write down this type of information. They were encouraged to write notes about the needs of particular children, actions observed, or special information from parents that would be of concern to all staff.

STEPS IN IMPLEMENTATION:

1. At a staff meeting the need for better sharing of information about children was discussed. This was important to help with consistency between morning and afternoon staff.
2. The staff log book was decided on, which would be different from the sign-in sheet or the general public information log which focused on routine details.
3. The book was placed in the staff lounge for staff to use. It was kept in the desk drawer when no one was writing in it or reading it to ensure confidentiality.

COMMENTS:

Teachers soon began to write notes to each other about things related to particular children. The method proved to be effective in alerting the afternoon staff and the director to needs and concerns. Separate logs for each class were later created since not all staff worked with all the children.

PROBLEM AREA: "WHERE IS THE DIRECTOR, ANYWAY?"

SPECIFIC INCIDENT:

The staff needed to be aware of the director's whereabouts at all times and the procedures for handling emergencies while the director was out of the building.

HOW WAS IT SOLVED?:

When the director left the building, a removable self-stick note was left next to the staff sign-in page of the sign-in book stating:

- destination
- approximate time of return
- phone number (if there was one) where director could be reached
- which staff member would handle any emergencies or questions in the director's absence

STEPS IN IMPLEMENTATION:

1. The staff was told about this new system at a staff meeting. The director explained a note would always be left in the same place anytime she left. If no note was posted, the director was in the building and could be reached using the intercom or phones.
2. The person left in charge was always notified before the director left. This position was rotated among all lead teachers who were interested. Each teacher was asked how she felt about the added responsibility. The director tried to utilize everyone who expressed willingness to be "on call." Each time the director had to be absent, a teacher was asked about covering for that specific time in case special classroom needs on that day conflicted with the added responsibility.
3. **The director must remember to remove the note upon returning!**

COMMENTS:

Since the building is very large, people often thought the director was gone when she was actually just in a classroom or at the other end of the building. Now, staff know where to check to see if the director is in or not. There has never been an emergency while the director was away, but it relieved people to know that someone was in charge in case of one.

Organization

PROBLEM AREA: <u>FILING BEGINNING OF THE YEAR FORMS</u>

SPECIFIC INCIDENT:
With seven different nursery school classes there were an overwhelming number of forms to file each fall. Since parents did not always indicate their child's class and days, a huge amount of time was spent looking up each child's group to correctly file the forms.

HOW WAS IT SOLVED?:
A color code was assigned to each group. For example:

- Monday, Wednesday, Friday - 9:00 was red
- Monday, Wednesday, Friday - 1:00 was green
- Tuesday, Thursday - 1:00 was purple, etc.

STEPS IN IMPLEMENTATION:
1. Purchase self-adhesive color coding labels in as many colors as needed. They are available at most office supply stores.
2. Before the forms were distributed at orientation, each teacher placed her color code in the upper right hand corner of her classes' forms using colored dots.
3. When the different forms began filtering back, each could be grouped by color very quickly and filed in the appropriate place.

COMMENTS:
To save money the coding could be done with felt tip markers.

PROBLEM AREA: TELEPHONE INTERRUPTIONS

SPECIFIC INCIDENT:

Many phone calls were received in the early morning when the teachers were very busy. Answering the phone took a lot of time away from the children.

HOW WAS IT SOLVED?:

An inexpensive answering machine was purchased and messages were recorded. For example, "The teachers are busy with the children now and will return your call as soon as possible," or "You may leave a message or call back between 1:00 p.m. and 3:00 p.m. " An emergency number was given.

STEPS IN IMPLEMENTATION:

1. Buy an answering machine (new or used) and record the message.
2. It is important to have an alternate phone number that parents can call in case of a real emergency. Locate an alternate person and/or number who is willing to accept emergency phone calls.
3. Instruct the staff to plug in the answering machine each morning when they arrive. They may elect to answer the phone if things are very quiet, but most prefer not to be interrupted when they are greeting parents and children and setting up activities.

COMMENTS:

The cost involved in buying a machine is small compared to the time and energy phone calls take away from teachers. Most calls are the concern of the director rather than the teachers. There are also machines available that allow one to hear the message as it is being recorded and offer the option of answering the call. Although it is more expensive, this option would be especially important if there were no alternate way of reaching the center by telephone.

PROBLEM AREA: FIRE DRILLS

SPECIFIC INCIDENT:

Fire drills required by the licensing department were often neglected.

HOW WAS IT SOLVED?:

The dates of fire drills were put on the monthly calendar for parents. This served as a needed reminder to staff as well as informing parents. Fire drills were added to the director's overall calendar for specific weeks (not the day) during the year. This provided a reminder at the beginning of the week to implement a drill.

STEPS IN IMPLEMENTATION:

1. The fire drill problem was discussed at a staff meeting.
2. The staff agreed to the need for a schedule. Based on the number of drills required by the licensing department, various weeks throughout the year were designated as fire drill weeks.
3. Teachers planned practices before the drill.

COMMENTS:

Special lessons were planned around fire drill dates, such as Smokey the Bear, field trips to the fire department, and holiday fire safety. Integrating lesson plans with the drills helped to avoid frightening the children and made the drills go more smoothly.

PROBLEM AREA: REMEMBERING COMMITMENTS AND EVENTS

SPECIFIC INCIDENT:

The director forgot to tell teachers about a special event until almost too late!

HOW WAS IT SOLVED?:

The director got rid of extra calendars and developed one master calendar for the center on which all pertinent information was recorded. A duplicate copy was made to be kept at home. The calendar at home enabled family members to know of the director's evening commitments. It was kept by the phone at home.

STEPS IN IMPLEMENTATION:

1. The director purchased a large, undated year-long wall calendar for center use.
2. The calendar was then covered with clear contact so mistakes could be wiped off or changes made as the year progressed. Plastic laminate could also be used. Additionally, it could be wiped clean and reused for another year.
3. The director wrote in the months and dates and worked with the staff to write in all known events. Each teacher chose a color to use for her schedule. The color codes were written on the calendar (i.e. a green noted event meant something scheduled for the toddler group). Black was chosen for all center events and for the director's notes about planning or other reminders.

COMMENTS:

It was very inefficient time usage to keep transferring information between calendars. Now that there are only two, it is easier to be prepared for commitments! The home calendar is a notebook type which can be brought to the office as needed for cross-checking.

PROBLEM AREA: DULL SNACK MENU

SPECIFIC INCIDENT:

Snack was not planned and became monotonous. A supply closet of crackers and cookies was available and that was what teachers served each day unless they had a special cooking project.

HOW WAS IT SOLVED?:

A snack schedule for the month was devised. Teacher ideas were utilized, which included cooking projects they had used with their children. Thus a variety of snack items were developed and it provided time for children to participate in snack preparation. Those snacks that did not work were crossed out and replace by new suggestions for the coming month.

STEPS IN IMPLEMENTATION:

1. At a staff meeting snacks were discussed and the possibility of planning a more interesting schedule was investigated.
2. The teachers described cooking activities that their children enjoyed and suggested that those participating in a cooking project might prepare enough for the whole school's snack.
3. The children were made aware of the snacks for the coming week and were allowed to choose the ones they would like to help prepare.

COMMENTS:

Staff developed the snack schedule from their curriculum plans. It was much easier to shop having this schedule to follow. The system worked very well and integrated a routine activity into the overall curriculum plan with delicious results.

PROBLEM AREA: KEEPING CURRENT

SPECIFIC INCIDENT:
The director needed time for professional reading.

HOW WAS IT SOLVED?:
The director scheduled time to read journals, magazine articles and related professional material one hour per week.

STEPS IN IMPLEMENTATION:
1. Set aside one regular day per week to come into work an hour late.
2. Stay at home and do nothing but read professional literature.
3. Allocate more time for this as special needs arise, such as conducting special staff training sessions or parent education programs.

COMMENTS:
The director is now able to keep current. Setting aside one hour at the end of the day doesn't work because it's hard to leave early. Information of special interest to staff or parents can be posted or otherwise reported. The director's ability to serve as a resource person to staff and parents certainly is facilitated by setting aside scheduled time to keep informed.

PROBLEM AREA: LAST MINUTE SCROUNGING

SPECIFIC INCIDENT:

Consumable items for group projects were frequently needed, but parents were not aware of the need. So the teachers and director often spent time at the last minute scrounging for styrofoam meat trays or other items to be used in special projects.

HOW WAS IT SOLVED?:

A classified ad column was inserted in the newsletter each month to let parents know about items that were needed, such as paint shirts, baby food jars, scrap paper, and so on.

STEPS IN IMPLEMENTATION:

1. The teachers were asked what items they might want in the coming month for special projects, and to particularly note any holiday or seasonal projects that would require scrap supplies.
2. A list was compiled and distributed to staff for additions and deletions. A few days "thinking time" was always allowed each month.
3. The list was typed into the newsletter under a regular title such as "December's Want-Ads" or "December's Wish List."

COMMENTS:

The items needed were frequently donated. Parents also would ask if there was a use for some items they had access to that weren't on the lists. It pays to let people know your needs!

PROBLEM AREA: DISTRIBUTING TAKE-HOME MATERIALS

SPECIFIC INCIDENT:

Parent volunteers and aides became frustrated looking for names on mailboxes to sort children's work. Most papers had only first names on them and the names on the mailboxes were in alphabetical order by last name.

HOW WAS IT SOLVED?:

All the mailboxes were reorganized to the alphabetical order of the child's first name. The last initial was added when several children had the same first name.

STEPS IN IMPLEMENTATION:

1. Make stickers or labels of all the children's first names and arrange them in alphabetical order.
2. Place on mailboxes covering up any names already on the box. Be sure to tell the children and parents about the new system so they can find their new mailboxes.
3. Instruct the teachers to continue to write just first names on children's paper, but to be sure to add last initials for those children having the same name.

COMMENTS:

The volunteers are not as frustrated and now the task of sorting papers takes little time. This plan saves trouble for the teacher too, since helpers are not so frustrated by the job and don't have to ask for help with names.

PROBLEM AREA: CANCELLATIONS

SPECIFIC INCIDENT:

After holding enrollment slots for children, there were still too many cancellations the first week of the school year. An additional problem involved holding slots for children who planned to be gone for a lengthy period of time.

HOW WAS IT SOLVED?:

The process of enrollment included a $25.00 "registration." A holding fee of $50.00 was also instituted for those presently enrolled. If the child was gone from the center four weeks or more with proper notification, but planned to return, the parents paid a $50.00 holding fee (per child) to hold the spot. This amount was credited toward tuition upon re-enrollment, but was not refundable if the parents changed their minds.

STEPS IN IMPLEMENTATION:

1. The director checked with other programs in the community to see what policies they had, and asked how successful the policies were.
2. This policy was implemented when a tuition increase was announced, and a half-day charge policy for "vacations" of three or fewer full weeks was instituted.
3. Parents were given a one-month written notice and the parents handbook was revised.

COMMENTS:

The system works wonderfully! Now the registration fee ($25.00) holds a future slot for a "new" child and the holding fee ($50.00) holds the slot for an "old" child.

PROBLEM AREA: SECURITY

SPECIFIC INCIDENT:

The staff needed to prevent the "wrong" person from trying to pick up a child.

HOW WAS IT SOLVED?:

Passes were issued to all parents and those authorized by parents to pick up a child. The parents must show a pass to the teacher before the child is released.

STEPS IN IMPLEMENTATION:

1. Decide on a card format.
2. Print the cards. Have the parents' information recorded on the pass.
3. Issue cards to parents. Keep a copy in the file.

COMMENTS:

This system helps new staff who have "closing duty" who are not yet familiar with all of the parents.

Children

PROBLEM AREA: <u>GRADUATING TO AN OLDER AGE GROUP</u>

SPECIFIC INCIDENT:

When a child graduated from a younger group to the next one, the former teacher frequently did not share important information with the new teacher regarding the child or the family.

HOW WAS IT SOLVED?:

An in-service was provided concerning transitions from one group to another. It stressed the need for strong communication links between the two teachers. The teachers were asked to develop a transition system that would facilitate the way children coped with the changes. Staff meetings were scheduled in which children in transition were the sole topic of discussion. The former teacher related information about the child's background, level of development and specific ways to best meet the needs of the child.

STEPS IN IMPLEMENTATION:

1. Acknowledge that transition time requires attention. Initiate a transition policy or system.
2. Evaluate the children's ability to cope with changes involved in the transition, paying particular attention to ways that it could be made less stressful.
3. Amend the transition policy if necessary. Notice a child's response to the transition and record those observations in the child's file.

COMMENTS:

Try to provide joint group activities so the children get to know the teacher they will "graduate" to. The teacher will also get an opportunity to observe the child and note any particular questions.

PROBLEM AREA: BITING

SPECIFIC INCIDENT:

One of the toddlers frequently bit the other children.

HOW WAS IT SOLVED?:

A collapsible playpen was used for toddler time-out after biting. Any biting incident was followed by placing the toddler in the playpen for two to three minutes. The toddler then recognized that she or he had been isolated from the peer group and was being disciplined.

STEPS IN IMPLEMENTATION:

1. The staff discussed how to deal with toddler biting since it could not always be prevented, despite efforts to do so.
2. The staff wanted a discipline technique that could be implemented immediately after the incident and one that a toddler could comprehend.
3. After a trial period which was successful, this system was written into the discipline policy.

COMMENTS:

It is important to have consistency. All staff must support and implement the policy or it won't work. The toddlers seem to understand the connection between biting and losing their freedom to play with their friends for a while.

PROBLEM AREA: LACK OF TODDLER FIELD TRIPS

SPECIFIC INCIDENT:

Parents complained that the toddlers weren't going on any field trips.

HOW WAS IT SOLVED?:

The bus rental company was asked to send separate seat belts to fasten two toddler car seats to each bus seat. Two metropolitan bus companies had these belts. The parents brought their toddler's car seat to the center on field trip days.

STEPS IN IMPLEMENTATION:

1. The director presented to staff the interest of parents in having trips for the toddlers. The toddler teachers also were interested in going on trips and were willing to try the car seat arrangements to make trips possible.
2. When toddler parents sign permission for a field trip they are asked to bring their child's car seat to school on the field trip day.
3. Allow a few extra minutes for one or two staff members to get the car seats set up before the children board.

COMMENTS:

The toddlers are so comfortable, they arrive at the destination rested and ready to go!

PROBLEM AREA: <u>NAPTIME ADJUSTMENT</u>

SPECIFIC INCIDENT:

One of the children was afraid of the dark and of the new naproom.

HOW WAS IT SOLVED?:

A nightlight was purchased, which was used in the section of the room where that child napped.

STEPS IN IMPLEMENTATION:

1. The staff discussed the problem. The teachers were concerned that the child was bothering others by crying and making it harder for staff to supervise the room.
2. It was decided that the fear was very real for the child and the staff brainstormed ways to handle it.
3. The nightlight idea was tried first. In addition, teachers stayed in the room a little longer until the child became used to the room.

COMMENTS:

The light worked very well. The area had enough light for the child, and the usual naproom environment was not significantly changed.

PROBLEM AREA: NEW CHILDREN AT THE CENTER

SPECIFIC INCIDENT:

New children often experience anxiety and confusion the first few days at the center.

HOW WAS IT SOLVED?:

A child in his/her class is assigned to be their helper for the day. This child helps the new child locate different areas in school and learn the rules. He or she also plays with the child during the day.

STEPS IN IMPLEMENTATION:

1. Introduce the new child to the entire class.
2. Assign a helper/friend from the class.
3. Remind the helper to show the child the bathroom, naproom, gym and other places used during the day.

COMMENTS:

This system makes the new child feel more at home, and gives the entire class a positive feeling about helping the child settle in. The children who are helpers feel a real sense of responsibility for helping the new child feel at home, thus learning valuable social skills. The staff asks for volunteer helpers, but usually everyone wants to be it, so now names are drawn from a hat or the staff uses their own judgment in selecting the helper. The child is asked if she or he would like to be the helper for the day and the child is free to decline. If necessary, helpers for the new child may be assigned for several days.

PROBLEM AREA: SCHEDULING NURSERY SCHOOL CLASSES FOR 3'S

SPECIFIC INCIDENT:

The 2½ - 3's had been attending on Tuesday and Thursday mornings. Teachers said that Thursdays went smoothly but each Tuesday was "like starting over again."

HOW WAS IT SOLVED?:

The staff decided there was too much time between Thursday and the following Tuesday, causing a constant readjustment problem. The decision was made to split the week more equally.

STEPS IN IMPLEMENTATION:

1. The entire school schedule was readjusted so that the 3's could come on Tuesday and Friday. This entailed having the older children (4's-5's) come Monday, Wednesday and Thursday instead of the more traditional Monday, Wednesday and Friday.

COMMENTS:

The change was made at the beginning of the school year so as not to disrupt people's existing schedules. The teachers of the older children enjoy having two consecutive days available to schedule some special projects.

PROBLEM AREA: ADJUSTMENT TO DAY CARE

SPECIFIC INCIDENT:

Many children and parents experience severe separation anxiety the first few times the child attends school.

HOW WAS IT SOLVED?:

Mom and/or Dad are required to attend one or more sessions to give their child needed support in the new situation, before regular attendance begins.

STEPS IN IMPLEMENTATION:

1. One parent attends a pre-orientation to day care by coming with their child for a normal morning session. They are encouraged to stay as long as they wish, but at least an hour visit is required for the parent and child.
2. If the child is willing, he or she is encouraged to join into the normal morning schedule.
3. At this time the child meets teachers and other children, and joins in free play, snacktime and group time. During this time mom or dad is present. This is not considered regular attendance, but is a specifically required orientation session.

COMMENTS:

The secret is not to use pressure. Let the child set the pace. This system has helped all children become comfortable by letting them know what to expect their first day. At this session, the staff can also detect children who may have more problems with separation and then additional parent visits can be suggested.

PROBLEM AREA: SPITTING & SWEARING

SPECIFIC INCIDENT:

Children were spitting and swearing at each other.

HOW WAS IT SOLVED?:

Specific limits were set and those unacceptable activities were redirected.

STEPS IN IMPLEMENTATION:

1. For swearing, the children were told that it was bathroom type language and if they wanted to swear they had to go swear in the bathroom. They had to throw those bad words into the toilet.
2. For spitting they were told that spitting had to be directed into something called a "spittoon" which could be the wastebasket, the toilet, or a paper cup if they were outside.
3. An alternate solution to the spitting problem involves an overcorrection technique in which the child is required to spit into the toilet numerous times.

COMMENTS:

At first children ran into the bathroom to exhibit these behaviors but soon they tired of doing that and stopped spitting and swearing. Initially, the policy was enforced by taking the children by the hand to the appropriate spot. Later they were sent on their own.

PROBLEM AREA: NO EXTRA CLOTHES

SPECIFIC INCIDENT:

Children needed a change of clothes but did not have one either because they had not replaced their extra set when it was used, or because they hadn't stored a spare set at school.

HOW WAS IT SOLVED?:

A supply of clothes belonging to the center was established, in addition to those that each child is requested to bring for himself or herself. They are kept in boxes labeled according to the type of clothing (i.e. pants, underwear, shirts, mittens, hats).

STEPS IN IMPLEMENTATION:

1. Petty cash was used to buy some clothes at garage sales for the center supply closet.
2. Staff and parents donated some of their children's outgrown clothes.
3. The children used the center clothes as needed, but if they wore them home parents were required to wash and return them within a week.

COMMENTS:

Spare clothes such as mittens, hats, and snowpants are not sent home since they are often not returned. Those items are kept at the center and washed as needed. A volunteer might be willing to embroider the center's name on all articles of clothing to increase the possibility of their return.

Parents

PROBLEM AREA: <u>PARENT INVOLVEMENT</u>

SPECIFIC INCIDENT:
The staff wanted to make parents a part of the holiday festivities at the center, but realized that most of them had very busy schedules.

HOW WAS IT SOLVED?:
The teachers had the children help make different holiday goodies and then recorded them singing their favorite holiday songs. A holiday open house for parents was arranged and they were invited to stop in at their leisure.

STEPS IN IMPLEMENTATION:
1. Have the children help make cookies and other goodies.
2. Record the children singing holiday songs.
3. Set up an open house area, including a tea tray of refreshments and a tape recorder to provide the background music.

COMMENTS:
Parents felt this was a special treat. It gave them time to stop at the center and spend some time with their child and teacher. They were able to come at their convenience, and the staff was able to be with parents a few at a time instead of having the pressure of a large holiday party with a performance by the children.

PROBLEM AREA: EXTRA HELP NEEDED

SPECIFIC INCIDENT:

The budget did not allow time or money for staff to do many necessary jobs, such as repairing toys, painting rooms, making copies, etc.

HOW WAS IT SOLVED?:

Parents were asked to volunteer.

STEPS IN IMPLEMENTATION:

1. A form was sent home with registration materials requesting information on the types of jobs for which parents would be willing to volunteer.
2. A card index was created for each project area with names of potential volunteers.
3. The staff, director and Board of Directors committee uses the index to find people willing to help on their projects.

COMMENTS:

If volunteer help is hard to obtain, consider occasionally making an adjustment on child care charges in exchange for work done in the center. In addition to parent volunteers, the local Voluntary Action Center may be of assistance in locating additional help, such as senior citizen groups, churches, government programs, etc.

PROBLEM AREA: THE SILENT MAJORITY

SPECIFIC INCIDENT:
The staff needed to get feedback from this very important group of parents.

HOW WAS IT SOLVED?:
Every spring a parent evaluation form is sent home allowing each family the opportunity to evaluate all aspects of the center.

STEPS IN IMPLEMENTATION:
1. An introduction to the survey is included which explains the importance of every family giving feedback about the program.
2. After receiving the forms (about 56% were returned), the data was compiled in two ways: (1) an overall tabulation for the center; (2) a tabulation by program grouping (nursery school, kindergarten enrichment program, school-age day care program). This allowed each staffing group to look at how they were doing, what they could feel good about, and what needed work.
3. A letter/report was written to all the parents giving the results of the survey and actions planned to solve problem areas.

COMMENTS:
The board receives all the data tabulation. Their committees use the information for setting goals and clarifying parents' needs and concerns. The director uses the data to set goals and administrative priorities.

PROBLEM AREA: MISPLACED CHILDREN'S CLOTHES

SPECIFIC INCIDENT:

Parents were not labeling their children's clothes. Then they complained when their child's clothes were misplaced.

HOW WAS IT SOLVED?:

Instead of just talking about the need to label their children's clothes, at the orientation each parent was handed an order blank for children's iron-on name labels. The importance of ordering and using these labels was stressed. When people would ask about lost clothes the staff would say, "If it had a name on it I'm sure we can find it."

STEPS IN IMPLEMENTATION:

1. Obtain the names of companies which make iron-on labels and ask them to send a batch of order blanks to distribute to parents.

COMMENTS:

Distributing order blanks makes it easier for parents to comply with the request.

PROBLEM AREA: DAILY COMMUNICATION ABOUT BEHAVIOR

SPECIFIC INCIDENT:

The staff wanted to inform parents about a child's behavior during the day.

HOW WAS IT SOLVED?:

Each staff member completes a form for the children in his or her group and puts it in the child's file to be picked up each day by the parents.

STEPS IN IMPLEMENTATION:

1. Develop forms including all the routine activities such as eating, sleeping, clean-up, and playing. Make the activities appropriate for the age groups (i.e. potty training for toddlers, but not on preschoolers' notes). Include a space for comments. A smiling face and a sad face are drawn next to each activity. Duplicate the forms.
2. The teachers complete one for each child by coloring in the appropriate face. The faces make these easy to use.
3. Remember to distribute them daily to parents.

COMMENTS:

The children really make an effort to get smiling faces on their notes. Parents are not surprised when the staff talks to them about a specific behavior concern because the notes have given them some prior warning of problems.

PROBLEM AREA: INFORMING PARENTS OF DAILY ACTIVITIES

SPECIFIC INCIDENT:

The parents frequently asked what their child did during the day.

HOW WAS IT SOLVED?:

A form was created for each group of children in which the teacher explained the day's activities.

STEPS IN IMPLEMENTATION:

1. Develop the forms.
2. The teachers are introduced to the form and shown how to use it.
3. The teachers hang the completed form on the parents' board.

COMMENTS:

So often when parents ask children, "What did you do today?" the reply is "Play." Whenever possible the teachers also suggested questions that parents could ask their children that were likely to yield better results. For example, "Tell me about the snack you made," "Show me how you pretended you were an airplane," or "Which things floated in the water table and which ones sank?"

PROBLEM AREA: ACKNOWLEDGING AND ENCOURAGING DONATIONS

SPECIFIC INCIDENT:

The staff wanted to publicly acknowledge donations to the center, in addition to thanking donors privately.

HOW WAS IT SOLVED?:

In the monthly newsletter for parents, there is a "Roses" column. Donations are listed there. "Roses to Susan Smith, Billy's Mom, for the computer paper." "Roses to Frank Jones, Missy's Dad, for the used children's books, dress-up clothes and magazines."

STEPS IN IMPLEMENTATION:

1. Ask the teachers to keep a list of donations given to their rooms.
2. Compile the list, double checking with teachers for accuracy.
3. Type it into the newsletter.

COMMENTS:

The column used to be called "Roses and Onions" and items which didn't help the center would be listed as "Onions." For example, "Onions to this month's weather which made us play indoors so often." The director had to eliminate the "Onions" part of the column, because after a few issues there were so many wonderful donations that the column got too long. The "Onions" idea was a good way of letting parents know about little problem areas with which the staff had to cope. It showed them that the center did the best in the face of adversity.

PROBLEM AREA: UNDELIVERED HANDOUTS

SPECIFIC INCIDENT:

Newsletters and memos, the primary method of communicating with parents about procedures and center information, were not being taken home for parents to read.

HOW WAS IT SOLVED?:

Each child's name was placed on the top of a handout so that lost handouts could be given to the proper family. A bulletin board section was initiated that read "We sent these handouts home this week, did you get one?"

STEPS IN IMPLEMENTATION:

1. Each parent was personally informed that important notices and memos would be put on the bulletin board for them to check. They were asked to make sure they had a copy. Each week's handouts were then posted in that section so parents could see what they should have received. Extra copies were available in the office.
2. The staff made a point to personally give out lost memos that were found.

COMMENTS:

The staff also stressed with the children the importance of taking notices home. They were told to ask for another one if something happened to theirs. The teachers also explained the newsletter to the children and told them something of interest to show their parents! To pique the parents' interest articles were often included in the newsletter that mentioned many children.

PROBLEM AREA: COMMUNICATING WITH PARENTS OF TODDLERS

SPECIFIC INCIDENT:

Parents were not reading the daily charts written by the teachers about each toddler. This was discouraging to the teachers and did not build good home-center communication, which the staff felt was important in the toddler program.

HOW WAS IT SOLVED?:

The sign-in sheet was posted next to the daily charts, and a check-off sheet was posted for them to indicate their toddler's daily chart had been read. A space was left on the check-off sheet for their comments.

STEPS IN IMPLEMENTATION:

1. Set up an attractive and noticeable area for these charts, daily sign-in sheets, and the toddler chart check list.
2. Point this out to the parents so they will see them and know they are supposed to read them and respond.

COMMENTS:

The parents were very pleased to read the charts once they got used to the system. They really liked finding out what had happened. They did make comments to the teacher when given space to do so.

PROBLEM AREA: PARENT NOTICES

SPECIFIC INCIDENT:

The staff wanted to notify parents of field trips and other important events.

HOW WAS IT SOLVED?:

A parent bulletin board was created on which daily news and notes were written to the parents by each classroom teacher. For special occasions a huge sheet of paper covers all the usual notes and states the information in large letters, such as, **"FIELD TRIP TODAY."**

STEPS IN IMPLEMENTATION:

1. In place of individual daily notes, the staff makes a large sign explaining the field trip or special activity. It is posted on the parent bulletin board.
2. The entrance door is also used to post special notices.

COMMENTS:

Parents can't miss the notice on these large signs, or can they?

PROBLEM AREA: INFORMING PARENTS OF UPCOMING EVENTS

SPECIFIC INCIDENT:

The director often found there was not enough time to do a newsletter, yet parents still needed to know about important upcoming events.

HOW WAS IT SOLVED?:

A large calendar was placed by the parents' board with all the monthly events on it (birthdays, weekly units, child of the week, field trips, holidays and parties).

STEPS IN IMPLEMENTATION:

1. Purchase a large calendar.
2. Write all the monthly events on it.
3. Remind the parents to read it.

COMMENTS:

Not only was there not always time to write a newsletter, it was also expensive because it had to be photocopied. The calendar provides parents all the needed information, plus it is in plain view where parents can see it and use it without losing it. Parents are reminded to write the dates they need to remember onto their own calendars.

PROBLEM AREA: SENDING PAPERS HOME

SPECIFIC INCIDENT:

The staff wanted to find an efficient and effective way to get messages to parents.

HOW WAS IT SOLVED?:

A file system was developed. Parents check the child's folder daily to pick up messages, newsletters, children's work, and so on.

STEPS IN IMPLEMENTATION:

1. Use a file box with hanging folders.
2. Place the childrens' files in alphabetical order, using the child's first name and last initial.
3. Keep next to the sign-in sheet.

COMMENTS:

If a parent does not use the file, a note is put on the sign-in sheet. The staff makes a point to remind parents to check the file for important messages. With this system the staff knows which parents have not received information and thus specific individuals can be contacted when necessary.

PROBLEM AREA: REPETITIVE PARENT QUESTIONS

SPECIFIC INCIDENT:

Parents were constantly asking many of the same questions about basic routines and guidelines. These had been outlined in the past through newsletters, conferences, and verbal communication.

HOW WAS IT SOLVED?:

To solve the problem of making sure that all parents received the same information regarding the school program, a "Parent Handbook" was devised. What started out as a few pages soon grew to over 20 pages. Areas covered included: Ground Rules, Suggestions for Separation, Daily Schedule, Objectives and Policies, Medical and Health Information, Snacks and Birthday Ideas, Special Events at School, and Yearly Activities. A special section was included for full-day children, covering lunches, naps, early arrival and late pickup. A glossary completed the book.

STEPS IN IMPLEMENTATION:

1. Ideas for the handbook came from previous communications, staff suggestions, newsletters and parent questions.
2. Some staff volunteered help on the parent handbook. The parent advisory committee members also helped.

COMMENTS:

Now when parents ask questions that are answered in the handbook, they are referred to the appropriate page in the handbook. In the newsletter, items in the handbook are often referred to.

PROBLEM AREA: WINTER OUTDOOR PLAY

SPECIFIC INCIDENT:

Some parents wanted their children to stay inside, while the staff felt all children needed to be outside.

HOW WAS IT SOLVED?:

A policy was written by the director and put in the *Parent Policies Handbook*.

STEPS IN IMPLEMENTATION:

1. Medical advice was obtained concerning when children should not go out.
2. The policy was written making parents responsible for proper clothing. Each family was given a copy of the *Parent Policies Handbook*.
3. The policy was enforced and extra clothing and boots were available when parents forgot.

COMMENTS:

The policy states that all children will go outside unless:

- the temperature is below 5 degrees
- the windchill is below -10 degrees
- the child is taking prescription medication

Having the extra clothes available (in cold climates) means the policy can be enforced by the school. The staff also checks for proper clothes on arrival and has at times requested that parents bring proper clothes to the school before outdoor time. The policy also discourages parents from sending to school children who are not healthy enough to play outside.

PROBLEM AREA: EARLY ARRIVALS

SPECIFIC INCIDENT:

Although school began at 9:00 a.m., some children were arriving as early as 8:15 a.m.

HOW WAS IT SOLVED?:

A drop-in fee policy was developed for before school. A parent letter was sent home notifying them that in response to apparent needs, drop-in child care would now be offered before school. The fee was $2.00 per hour or portion thereof, and would apply to all children arriving more than 5-10 minutes before school. If parents had special needs or questions they were requested to call the director.

STEPS IN IMPLEMENTATION:

1. A notice was sent home regarding the new policy.
2. The bookkeeper and teachers were informed of the new policy. Teachers were asked to keep track of any children who came early and report this to the bookkeeper. Small memo pads were used to indicate the child's name and time of arrival.
3. A starting date was set for the new policy so it could begin after proper notice. The director had the bookkeeper check with her before actually adding fees to any parent's bill so the director could talk to the parents if it seemed appropriate.

COMMENTS:

This policy could also work for children who are not picked up on time. The letter can be worded in a supportive way, stressing concern about children being left unsupervised if teachers are not there and the need to have a staff person available for any children who come before the teachers may be available. Explain that teachers frequently have special conferences or staff meetings before school which make them unavailable to the children.

PROBLEM AREA: DEPARTURE

SPECIFIC INCIDENT:

A problem existed with children being picked up after the closing hour. One child was picked up one hour after closing time.

HOW WAS IT SOLVED?:

An overtime fee was initiated. Parents pay staff, on the spot, a $2.00 late fee for every 15 minutes or fraction thereof. Information on how to deal with late pickups is included in the employee handbook. The director carefully explains the policy to new staff working the closing shift.

STEPS IN IMPLEMENTATION:

1. Decide on a rate with the staff. Rates vary from $2.00 to $2.50 for 5 to 15 minutes late. An average charge for an hour late is $8.00 to $10.00.
2. Inform parents through a policy/parent handbook. Specifically state the policy in person to parents at the enrollment session. Specify that the money is to be paid directly to the staff person at the time.
3. Encourage the staff to enforce the policy. A late pick-up form was developed which the teacher fills out and gives to the parent. Suggest that they tactfully explain that this is the late fee statement and to please reimburse them. Occasionally a parent is billed if they do not have the money with them.

COMMENTS:

If a parent calls with some special emergency circumstance that has only happened one time and involves a late pickup, a charge is not made. Chronic offenders are warned a few times, and may be asked to make other child care arrangements. Or they may be told that the next time it occurs the staff will be instructed to call the police and an abandoned child report will be filed. (So far it has never happened!) Parents seem to respond very effectively to closing time limits when money is involved.

PROBLEM AREA: PARENTS MISUNDERSTANDING POLICIES

SPECIFIC INCIDENT:

Parents were sometimes pleading ignorance of center rules and policies.

HOW WAS IT SOLVED?:

A "Parent Contract" was created which was discussed with the parents and signed during their initial visits. All important rules and policies were included on the contract form.

STEPS IN IMPLEMENTATION:

1. Create a contract and have it printed. Get input from the staff on important items to include.
2. Review the contract with parents during the center registration interview.
3. Have the parent sign the form, then file it in the center's file.

COMMENTS:

Parents can no longer say that they were never told about the center policies. The director no longer has to make personal judgments about excuses.

PROBLEM AREA: LATE PAYMENT OF TUITION

SPECIFIC INCIDENT:

Parents were chronically late in paying tuition. The director was expending a lot of energy asking parents about tuition payments.

HOW WAS IT SOLVED?:

Tuition was set $5.00 higher per week and a discount of $5.00 was granted to those paying in advance. Tuition was listed as $55.00 per week, but it was actually $50.00 per week if paid in advance or no later than Monday of the week.

STEPS IN IMPLEMENTATION:

1. Tuition rate sheets explaining the new tuition policy were written.
2. Parents were given a two-week notice so they could plan their other bills, thus allowing them to take advantage of the new policy.

COMMENTS:

Parents were more likely to pay in advance since they felt they were getting a bargain rather than being penalized for late payment.

PROBLEM AREA: SCHEDULING PARENT CONFERENCES

SPECIFIC INCIDENT:

It was hard to schedule conferences in the evening because teachers and parents were both very tired. It took a great deal of the director's time to schedule conferences, and parents would frequently cancel.

HOW WAS IT SOLVED?:

Conferences were scheduled during the day, at drop-off time, over lunch hour, during naptime, or in the late afternoon. Parents were asked to fill out forms indicating the time of day they preferred. Then a schedule was set up reflecting the times parents had chosen.

STEPS IN IMPLEMENTATION:

1. Develop a note to send to parents requesting them to choose a time of day.
2. Confirm their appointment with a return form that says "Yes, I can come" or "No, please reschedule for ________ at ________."
   date time
3. Hire substitutes or use a floater-staff person to cover for teachers as they are holding conferences.

COMMENTS:

The option of evening was available for those who wished, but most people preferred day-time conferences, as did the staff. This system was more efficient because there were very few cancellations and staff didn't feel burdened with extra evenings of work. Parents also didn't linger as long since they had to get back to work or were anxious to go home, so the time spent in the conference was more productive.

PROBLEM AREA: SCHEDULING PART-TIME CHILDREN

SPECIFIC INCIDENT:

Parents were constantly asking if their child could come on Wednesday instead of Tuesday this week or make other changes in their schedule.

HOW WAS IT SOLVED?:

A paired partner system for all part-time children was developed so that parents negotiated with each other. That made each family responsible for the portion of a slot for which they had enrolled their child. This helped meet the parents' need for some flexibility without putting the added burden on the staff.

STEPS IN IMPLEMENTATION:

1. After registration, a letter is sent to each family confirming their child's schedule.
2. Parents sign a contract to pay for the days and times for which they have enrolled their child.
3. If one child attends Monday, Wednesday, and Friday and another attends Tuesday and Thursday, the two families are considered to share one full-time slot and can negotiate any changes between themselves.
4. Parents are informed in writing of the family with whom they share a full-time slot.

COMMENTS:

If parents want to switch the days their child attends, they contact each other and arrange a trade, eliminating the need for the director to be involved in juggling bookkeeping or checking for room. All part-time children "share" their slot with another child and the parents are made aware of their partner. Parents making a switch are requested to send a note to the teacher letting her know. To implement this system part-time parents are now asked how flexible their schedules are and it is noted on their forms. An attempt is made to match people who need or want flexibility.

PROBLEM AREA: SCHEDULE CHANGES

SPECIFIC INCIDENT:

Some part-time enrollees requested an extra day, but the staffing pattern only allowed it if other children were absent. The potentially cumbersome bookkeeping task to make this accommodation seemed overwhelming.

HOW WAS IT SOLVED?:

Parents now call in when their child is going to be absent, thus allowing another chid to attend that day. The parents directly reimburse each other. The parent whose child was absent is responsible for collecting the fee.

STEPS IN IMPLEMENTATION:

1. Parents were informed of the possibility of implementing a reimbursement system. It was pointed out that the director would only be a catalsyst in the process and would not take on any extra work or expense for the bookkeeper or staff.
2. A simple form was developed to use in exchanging necessary information. One dollar was deducted from the reimbursement amount to help pay for the center's ordering of carbonless triplicate forms.
3. The form stated the name and address of the parent using extra time, the name and address of the parent to be reimbursed, and the amount owed. A copy is given to each parent and one is kept in a central file for parents to check in case a form gets lost.

COMMENTS:

Giving parents an option for reimbursement has been quite effective and has reduced complaints about having to pay for times their child was sick or had to be absent for a short time.

PROBLEM AREA: LATE TUITION PAYMENTS

SPECIFIC INCIDENT:

Families were not paying the weekly tuition on time and there were no consequences for this behavior.

HOW WAS IT SOLVED?:

A late fee of $1.00 per day was charged after a five day grace period. Payment was due Monday so if the payment wasn't in by the following Monday morning, the family accrued a $1.00 per day late fee in addition to the regular tuition.

STEPS IN IMPLEMENTATION:

1. Notify the parents and bookkeeper of the new policy, allowing two weeks before the policy is instituted.
2. Inform the staff about the new policy.
3. Begin the new policy.

COMMENTS:

Late fees can mount up quickly when charged on a daily basis. Most families pay on time or within the 5-day grace period.

PROBLEM AREA: <u>SCHEDULING NURSERY SCHOOL CLASSES</u>

SPECIFIC INCIDENT:

Some parents wanted a two-day program while others wanted a three-day program.

HOW WAS IT SOLVED?:

A basic two-day program is offered with an optional third day available.

STEPS IN IMPLEMENTATION:

1. The parents were assured that children would not miss anything major (parties, field trips, etc.) if they only attended two days a week.
2. A slight financial break was offered for children attending three days a week.
3. Parents had to commit themselves to the third day on a regular basis for staffing purposes, but some consideration was given to those wishing to add it after the year began.

COMMENTS:

Occasionally it has been necessary to rearrange the schedule. For instance, children who usually come Monday and Wednesday are asked to come Monday and Thursday if a field trip cannot be arranged on a Wednesday. This option has gradually increased the popularity of the three-day week program.

Environment

PROBLEM AREA: TOYS ACCESSIBLE AT WRONG TIMES

SPECIFIC INCIDENT:

Puzzles were all over the place when it was supposed to be story time.

HOW WAS IT SOLVED?:

Cabinets with doors were purchased. Other open cabinets were covered with fabric.

STEPS IN IMPLEMENTATION:

1. New cupboards that close were purchased.
2. For others, yards of cloth were bought and hemmed.
3. Covers were draped over open cupboards when toys were off limits.

COMMENTS:

The policy is "out of sight, out of mind." This way the children aren't tempted. They know they are not allowed to play with the toys when the cupboards are closed.

PROBLEM AREA: MISSING PUZZLE PIECES

SPECIFIC INCIDENT:

Puzzle pieces from both rubber and wooden puzzles were missing.

HOW WAS IT SOLVED?:

Many puzzles were salvaged by making replacement pieces.

STEPS IN IMPLEMENTATION:

- **To make wooden pieces:** Line the area of the puzzle, from which the piece is missing, with plastic food wrap. Fill with wood putty or plastic wood. When dry, remove by lifting out by the plastic food wrap. Color the piece with permanent felt tip markers and finish with a coat of clear sealer or lacquer.
- **To make rubber pieces:** Use the background and pieces from one of the puzzles that has numerous missing pieces to make the replacements for other puzzles. Trace an outline of the missing piece onto the rubber; cut out with a sharp razor blade or exacto knife.

COMMENTS:

Previously the staff had painted the replacement pieces for wood puzzles, but permanent felt tip markers work better and are available in a large assortment of colors. Some parents who have woodworking skills may volunteer to cut wood pieces with a jigsaw.

PROBLEM AREA: TOY STORAGE

SPECIFIC INCIDENT:

More classroom shelving was needed for manipulatives.

HOW WAS IT SOLVED?:

A puzzle center on wheels was created that could be moved from one area to another.

STEPS IN IMPLEMENTATION:

1. An old TV stand was obtained for use as a puzzle center.
2. Puzzle racks were placed on the stand. It was just the right size for two racks placed back to back.
3. The puzzle center could be set up in any part of the room by rolling the TV stand to that area.

COMMENTS:

It worked particularly well when the tables were being used for other purposes or when some children needed to work with puzzles in a separate area, rather than participate in a large group activity.

PROBLEM AREA: SPILLED PAINT

SPECIFIC INCIDENT:
Children were having accidents reaching to the center of the table for paints. Some children got upset when others mixed up colors in the central muffin tin paint holders.

HOW WAS IT SOLVED?:
Individual student paint palettes were made from styrofoam egg cartons.

STEPS IN IMPLEMENTATION:
1. Styrofoam egg cartons were collected.
2. Each egg carton was cut into thirds so that each piece had 4 holders to be used for the paint palette. The tops of the carton were removed or retained to use as covers, depending on childrens' ages. Older children could handle covers but they got in the way for younger children.
3. A small amount of different colored paint was poured into each cup of the egg carton paint palettes for each child's individual use. Cotton swabs or small-sized paint brushes were easier to use with these palettes. Brushes were also made by using bits of sponge held by plastic clip clothespins.

COMMENTS:
Carton palettes can be saved and rinsed out for reuse. When they get bent or coated with paint traces, throw them out and make new ones.

PROBLEM AREA: CRAYON/MARKER STORAGE

SPECIFIC INCIDENT:

A more efficient way was needed to sort and store crayons and colored markers since they were constantly being mixed up.

HOW WAS IT SOLVED?:

Color-coded containers were made from milk cartons.

STEPS IN IMPLEMENTATION:

1. Half-gallon milk cartons were cleaned, dried, and cut down in size to form squatty boxes.
2. The outsides were covered with colored construction paper to match the color of the markers or crayons it would contain.
3. If desired, these containers can then be covered with clear contact paper to make them more durable.

COMMENTS:

This became a good color matching activity. The ease of accessibility saved time for teachers and aides. Children could always find the colors they wanted to use and return them to the right place.

PROBLEM AREA: COSTLY EASEL PAINTS

SPECIFIC INCIDENT:
Commercial easel paints can be runny and are so expensive.

HOW WAS IT SOLVED?:
A homemade easel paint was used.

STEPS IN IMPLEMENTATION:
1. Make a thin white sauce by mixing 1 Tbsp. oil, 1 Tbsp. flour and 1 cup water. Cook over medium heat and stir constantly. Add 1 tsp. powdered tempera paint and 1 drop oil of wintergreen.
2. Refrigerate and store in a covered container.
3. Lasts about two weeks.

COMMENTS:
Dreft detergent can also be used as a paint extender by adding it to powdered tempera paint and water. Paint washes out of clothes easier because of the addition of the detergent.

PROBLEM AREA: SMELLY BATHROOMS

SPECIFIC INCIDENT:

The bathrooms developed an unpleasant urine smell toward the middle of the afternoon. This was undesirable not only for the staff and the children, but for parents and others visiting the center later in the day.

HOW WAS IT SOLVED?:

The bathroom was cleaned with a bleach solution each naptime.

STEPS IN IMPLEMENTATION:

1. The problem was discussed with staff at a staff meeting. Although bathrooms were cleaned every day after school by a janitorial service, staff agreed it was a serious problem during the day.
2. Midday cleaning was decided upon and staff were assigned, on a rotating basis, to clean bathrooms during naptime.
3. The bathroom surfaces were doused with a solution of 2 Tablespoons bleach to 1 gallon of water. Extra solution was mopped up. The cleaning service was asked to use the same solution.

COMMENTS:

The bleach kills the germs and urine smell and is economical. This procedure can be repeated a second time during the day if needed.

PROBLEM AREA: STATIC CLING

SPECIFIC INCIDENT:

Styrofoam packing peanuts were great in the indoor sandbox, but static cling made them unmanageable at clean-up time during the long, dry winter months.

HOW WAS IT SOLVED?:

This problem was minimuzed by putting fabric softener dryer sheets in the bottom of the styrofoam pile.

STEPS IN IMPLEMENTATION:

1. Bought fabric softener dryer sheets.
2. Staff used the sheets as needed to avoid static cling.
3. During clean-up at the end of the day, sheets were thrown away.

COMMENTS:

Judgement should be used in deciding the minimum age of children for whom this activity is appropriate. The possible danger of a young child biting into a piece of styrofoam and then choking necessitates close supervision in some situations.

PROBLEM AREA: FLIMSY MAILBOXES

SPECIFIC INCIDENT:

The children's milk carton "mailboxes" were not durable enough

HOW WAS IT SOLVED?:

Individual metal mailboxes were created.

STEPS IN IMPLEMENTATION:

1. Parents were asked to save three pound coffee cans.
2. Clusters of 10 cans were joined together with a pop riveter.
3. The cluster of cans were spray painted and hung on a wall near the coat hooks. An individual child's name was put on each mailbox can.

COMMENTS:

These looked very attractive and were much sturdier. Most take-home items could be rolled up easily to fit in the cans. **Hint:** Tape names on the upper half of the cans. When cans are loaded with materials, names on the bottoms of the cans are covered up.

PROBLEM AREA: SMELLY DIAPER PAIL

SPECIFIC INCIDENT:
The toddler area pail developed an unpleasant odor toward the middle of the day.

HOW WAS IT SOLVED?:
Orange peels were placed in the diaper pail so the smell became one of oranges rather than dirty diapers.

STEPS IN IMPLEMENTATION:
1. The director informed the staff and cook of the need for orange peels.
2. Anytime oranges are served for snack, the peels are saved in a bag in the refrigerator.
3. Peels are placed in the bottom of the diaper pail and replaced every other day.

COMMENTS:
Also try sprinkling baking soda. Be sure to spray the area with room freshener periodically.

PROBLEM AREA: COSTLY PAPER PRODUCTS

SPECIFIC INCIDENT:

The constant and necessary use of paper products by the children had a large impact on the supply budget.

HOW WAS IT SOLVED?:

An annual (or as often as necessary) center paper drive is held, and families are asked to contribute paper products of their choice (paper towels, toilet paper, facial tissues).

STEPS IN IMPLEMENTATION:

1. Advertise and set up "Drive Week."
2. Provide a container in the center for donations and a sheet upon which parents can record their contributions.
3. Be sure to thank everyone for their contributions.

COMMENTS:

This is a fun event, and gives families on even the tightest budget an opportunity to donate needed items to the center.

PROBLEM AREA: EXPENSIVE PAPER NAPKINS

SPECIFIC INCIDENT:

It seemed to be a waste of money to use large-sized napkins at snack and meal time.

HOW WAS IT SOLVED?:

Senior volunteers and special education volunteers cut the napkins in half, then refold them.

STEPS IN IMPLEMENTATION:

1. Purchase large-sized napkins.
2. Set up a work area and assign volunteers to the task.
3. Keep a basket handy to hold the ready supply of cut and folded napkins.

COMMENTS:

It offers volunteers an easy and constructive job that helps the center. The children can still practice good table manners using proper napkins, and the cost of supplies has been decreased.

PROBLEM AREA: SANDBOX

SPECIFIC INCIDENT:
A cover was needed for the plastic indoor sandbox.

HOW WAS IT SOLVED?:
A wooden box that enclosed the entire sandbox was made. Handles were added on the sides so the children could lift it themselves.

STEPS IN IMPLEMENTATION:
1. A volunteer grandfather built the lid for the cost of materials.
2. The lid was painted with green enamel and brown roads were painted on it for use with small cars and a village set.

COMMENTS:
Four positive results came from one solution: a volunteer became involved, the children are able to handle the sandbox on their own, an additional play surface was created and the sandbox now has a cover!

PROBLEM AREA: TAKING ITEMS OUTSIDE

SPECIFIC INCIDENT:

Nothing was very convenient for outdoor use. The staff was constantly running back and forth to get items such as facial tissues, extra spoons or shovels for sandbox, and balls.

HOW WAS IT SOLVED?:

A wagon was used to bring items back and forth thus eliminating many staff trips.

STEPS IN IMPLEMENTATION:

1. The wagon is loaded before going outside. Facial tissues, cars, trucks, equipment parts, special project needs, and balls are placed in the wagon.
2. The children are asked to think of things they use outside that can be remembered before going out.
3. Two children push and pull the wagon out to the yard. It is reloaded again when it is time to come in.

COMMENTS:

The system works very well. Children are involved in the process of planning for outdoors and are less prone to keep asking for extra things that are not outside.

PROBLEM AREA: SHARED SPACE

SPECIFIC INCIDENT:

A Monday program was not possible because the morning was spent setting up the classrooms which were also used as church school rooms.

HOW WAS IT SOLVED?:

Teenagers were hired to set up the rooms on Sunday evenings.

STEPS IN IMPLEMENTATION:

1. Initially the director supervised the youths as they set up the classroom.
2. The teachers drew diagrams of their rooms and each week noted for the teenagers any special requests concerning the set up.

COMMENTS:

Teachers are grateful to come in Monday morning to a prepared room. The teens work for a nominal amount and do the work more quickly than the teachers did! This plan saved wear and tear on staff, not to mention the director's back!

Afterword

We hope that you have enjoyed reading the information and ideas in this book. Support is greatly needed for all child care center directors, so we encourage you to share a few of your problem-solving ideas with a peer.

OTHER HELPFUL BOOKS PUBLISHED BY TOYS 'N THINGS PRESS

All Season Fun & Frolic — Indoor and outdoor activities for toddlers to school age.

Kids Encyclopedia of Things to Make and Do — Nearly 2,000 art and craft projects for children aged 4-10.

Open the Door, Let's Explore — Full of fun, inexpensive neighborhood walks and field trips designed to help young children.

Teachables From Trashables — Step-by-step guide to making over 50 fun toys from recycled household junk.

Teachables II — Similar to above; with another 75-plus toys.

Staff Orientation in Early Childhood Programs — Complete manual for orienting new staff on all program areas.

Forms Kit for Directors — Over 150 reproducible forms covering every need in an early childhood program.

S.O.S. Kit for Directors — Offers range of brainstormed solutions to everyday questions and problems.

Field Trips — Training guide full of ideas for trips, pre- and post-trip activities.

For You, For Them — Trainer bibliography of audio-visual and print resources in 6 topic areas.

Infant-Toddler Growth and Development — Helps trainers promote better understanding of normal development and what's appropriate.

New Faces, New Spaces: Helping Children Cope With Change — Training guide to better work with parents and caregivers.